The Mother Goose

Songbook

Nursery Rhymes to Play and Sing

Arranged for the piano by Carol Barratt

Illustrated by Jacqueline Sinclair

DERRYDALE BOOKS

NEW YORK

For Jody, Naomi, Leon and Charles

The chord symbols suggested have been chosen to suit the solo
melody and do not always correspond with the harmony of the
arrangement, as importance has been placed on interesting lef
hand accompaniments using simple hand positions. A chart
showing fingerings for guitar can be found at the back of
this book.

Musical arrangements copyright © 1984 by J & W Chester/Edition Wilhelm
Hansen London Ltd
Illustrations copyright © 1984 by Jacqueline Sinclair

This 1986 edition is published by Derrydale Books, distributed by Crown
Publishers, Inc., 225 Park Avenue South, New York, New York 10003
by arrangement with William Heinemann Ltd

Manufactured in Belgium

Library of Congress Cataloging-in-Publication Data

The Mother Goose songbook.

   Summary: A collection of twenty-eight nursery rhymes
with easy-to-play piano accompaniment.
   1. Children's songs.   2. Piano music—Juvenile.
3. Nursery rhymes.   [1. Nursery rhymes.   2. Songs]
I. Barratt, Carol.   II. Sinclair, Jacqueline, ill.
M1997.M919   1986   86-751108
ISBN 0-517-61575-4

h g f e d c

Contents

1   *Tom, Tom the Piper's Son*

Tom, Tom the pi – per's son, Stole a __ pig and a – way did run. The

pig was eat and Tom was beat, And Tom went_ howl-ing down the street.

2   I Had a Little Nut Tree

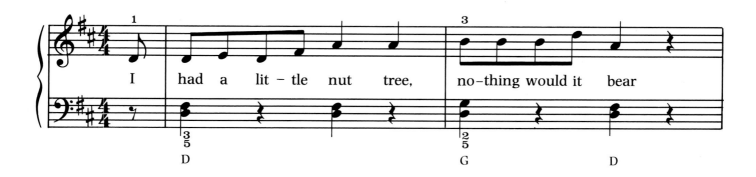

I had a little nut tree, nothing would it bear
But a silver nutmeg and a golden pear.
I skipped over water, I danced over sea,
And all the birds in the air couldn't catch me.

3   *Sing a Song of Sixpence*

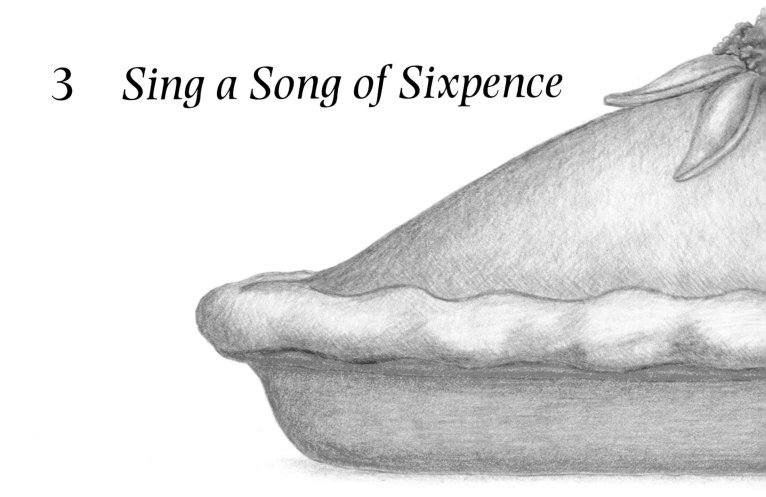

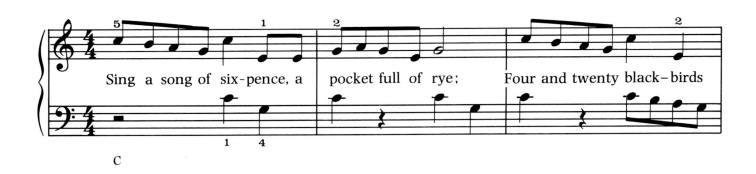

Sing a song of six-pence, a | pocket full of rye; | Four and twenty black-birds

C

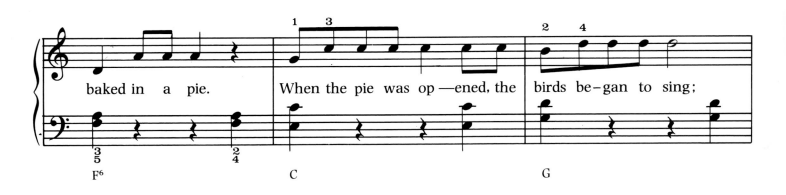

baked in a pie. | When the pie was op—ened, the | birds be-gan to sing;

F⁶   C   G

Was-n't that a dain-ty dish to set be—fore the King? (v. 2 The)

C   F   G   C

The King was in his counting house, counting out his money;
The Queen was in the parlor, eating bread and honey.
The maid was in the garden, hanging out the clothes,
When down came a blackbird, and pecked off her nose.

4 *Ride a Cock-Horse*

5 *The Mulberry Bush*

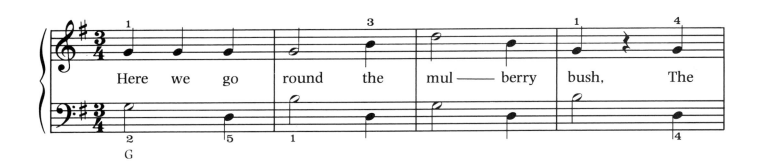

Here we go round the mul——berry bush, The

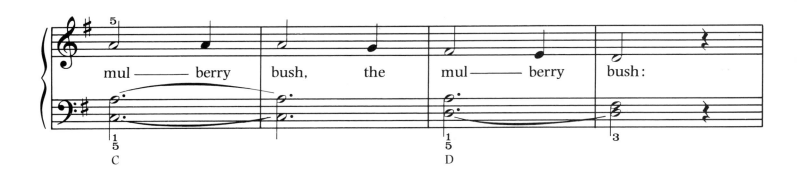

mul——berry bush, the mul——berry bush:

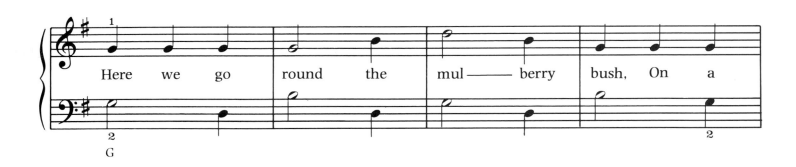

Here we go round the mul——berry bush, On a

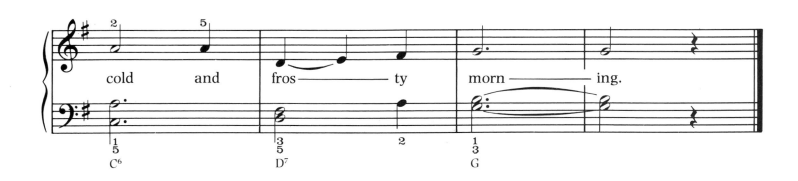

cold and fros——ty morn————ing.

This is the way we wash our hands . . .

This is the way we wash our clothes . . .

This is the way we dry our clothes . . .

This is the way we iron our clothes . . .

This is the way we sweep the floor . . .

This is the way we brush our hair . . .

This is the way we go to school . . .

This is the way we come back from school . . .

6 Ring-a-Ring o' Roses

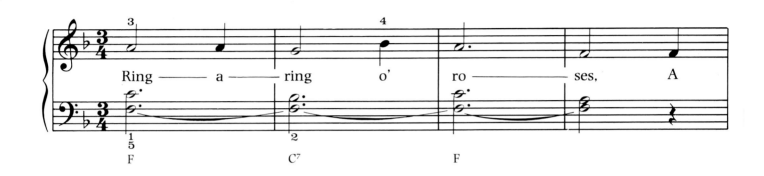

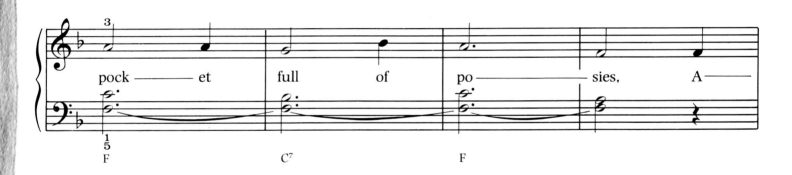

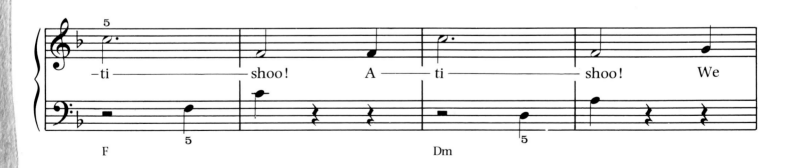

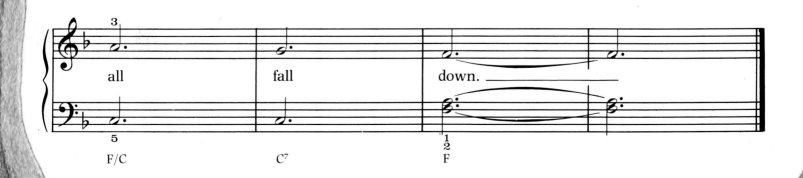

7   *Jack Sprat*

Jack   Sprat could   eat   no   fat,   His   wife could eat   no   lean;   And

G   C⁶   G   D

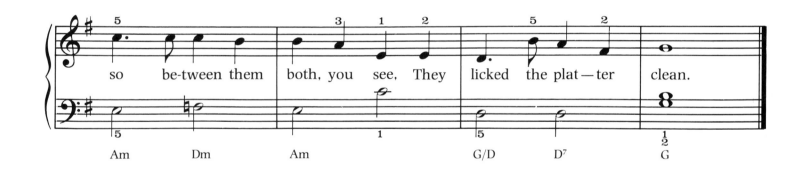

so   be-tween them   both, you   see, They   licked   the plat—ter   clean.

Am   Dm   Am   G/D   D⁷   G

8 One, Two, Three, Four, Five

One, two, / three, four, five, / Once I caught a / fish a—live,

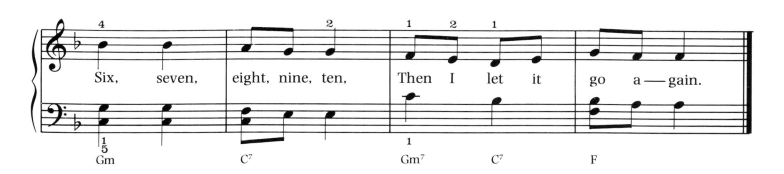

Six, seven, / eight, nine, ten, / Then I let it / go a—gain.

Why did you let it go?
Because it bit my finger so.
Which finger did it bite?
This little finger on the right.

9 Hickory, Dickory, Dock!

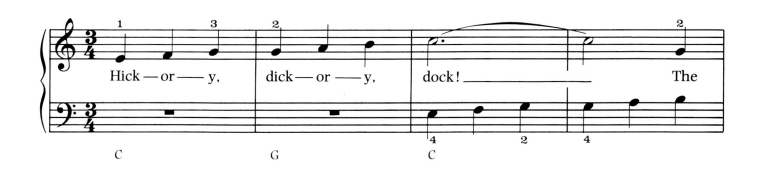

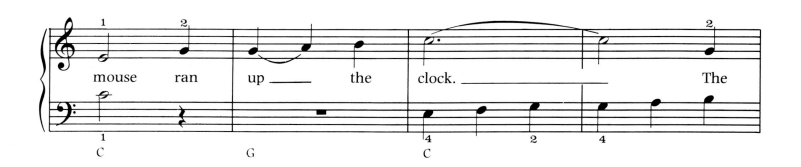

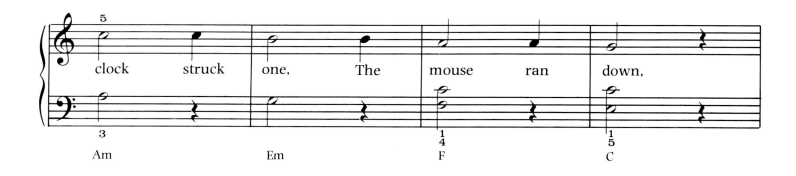

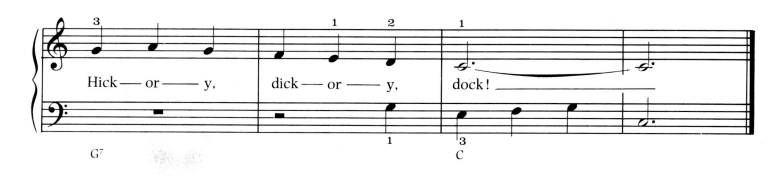

10 *Pat-a-Cake*

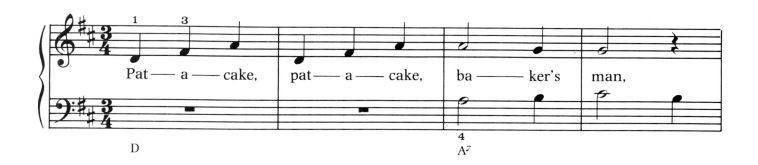

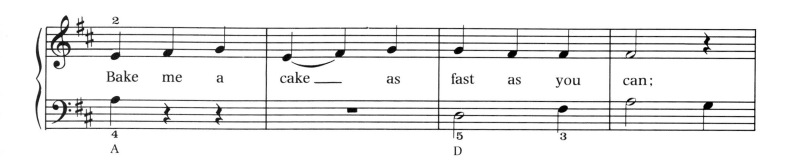

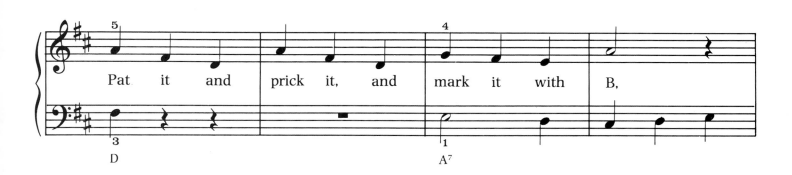

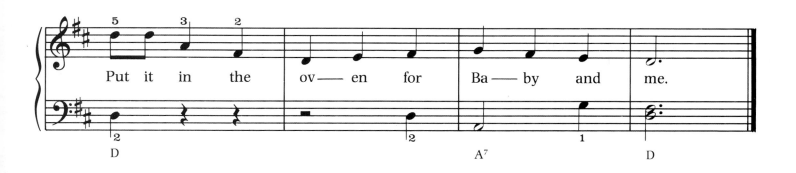

11 *London's Burning*

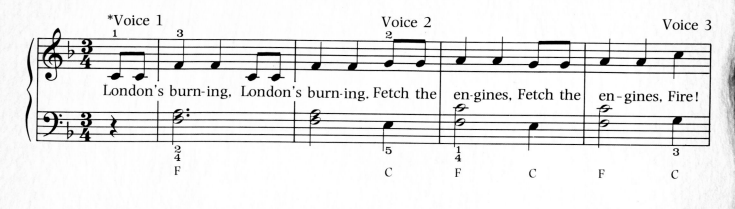

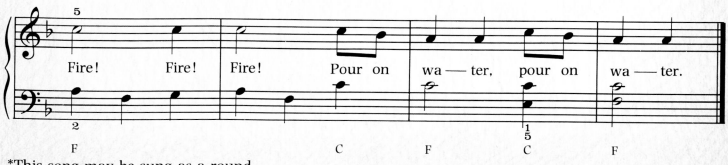

*This song may be sung as a round

12 Aiken Drum

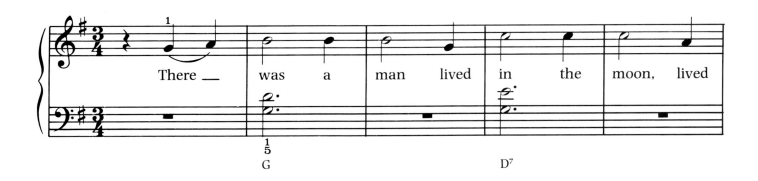

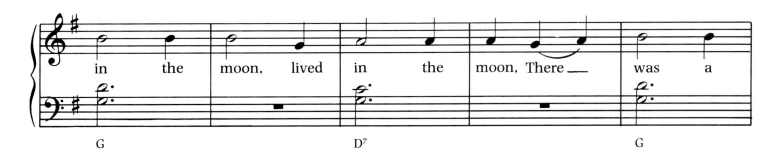

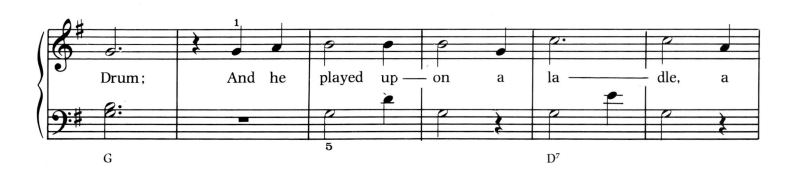

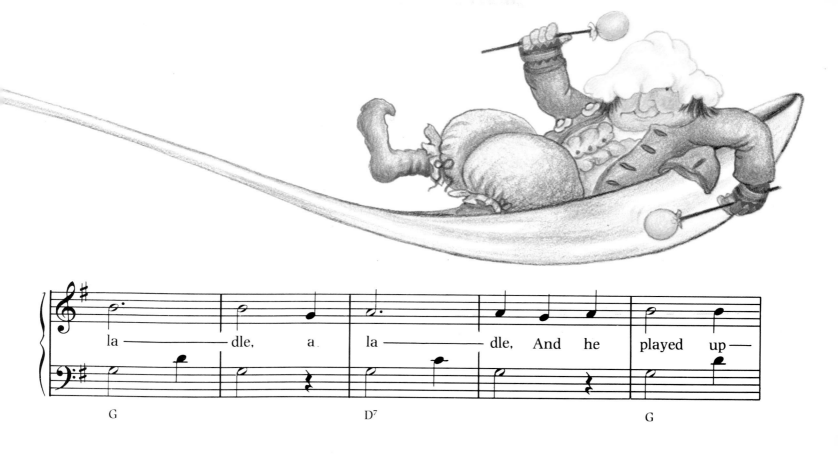

la —— dle, a la —— dle, And he played up—

G   D⁷   G

—on a la —— dle, And his name was Ai—ken Drum.

G   D⁷   G   D⁷   G

And his hat was made of good cream cheese . . .
And his name was Aiken Drum;
   And he played . . .

And his coat was made of good roast beef . . .
And his name was Aiken Drum;
   And he played . . .

And his buttons were made of penny loaves . . .
And his name was Aiken Drum;
   And he played . . .

His waistcoat was made of crust of pies . . .
And his name was Aiken Drum;
   And he played . . .

His breeches were made of haggis bags . . .
And his name was Aiken Drum;
   And he played . . .

13 Lavender's Blue

La——ven—der's blue, did–dle, did–dle, La——ven—der's green;

D   G/D

When I am king, did–dle, did—dle, You shall be queen.

D   A⁷   D

Call up your men, diddle, diddle,
Set them to work,
Some to the plow, diddle, diddle,
Some to the cart.

Some to make hay, diddle, diddle,
Some to cut corn,
Whilst you and I, diddle, diddle,
Keep ourselves warm.

Roses are red, diddle, diddle,
Violets are blue;
If you love me, diddle, diddle,
I will love you.

Let the birds sing, diddle, diddle,
And the lambs play;
We shall be safe, diddle, diddle,
Out of harm's way.

14 Oranges and Lemons

Or – an – ges and le – mons, Say the bells of St. Cle – ment's. You

F   C7   F

owe me five far – things, Say the bells of St. Mar – tin's.

F   C7   F

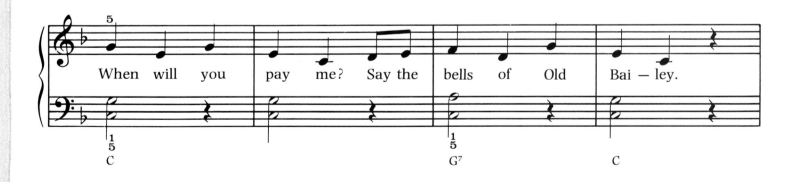

When will you pay me? Say the bells of Old Bai – ley.

C   G7   C

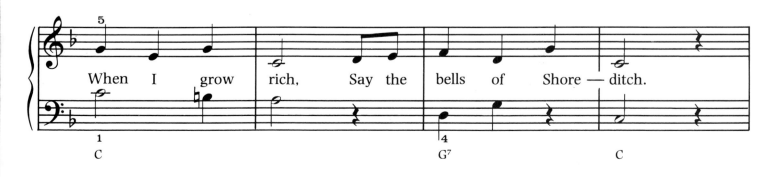

When I grow rich, Say the bells of Shore — ditch.

C   G7   C

15   Girls and Boys Come Out to Play

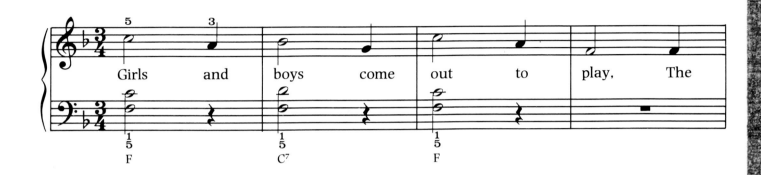

Girls and boys come out to play, The

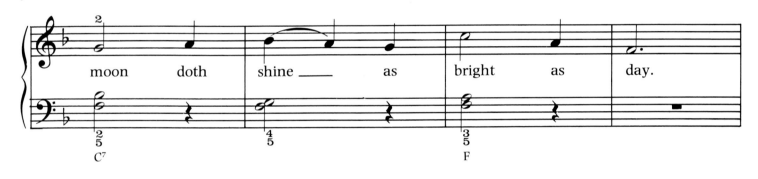

moon doth shine _____ as bright as day.

Leave your sup — per and leave your sleep, And
join your play — fel — lows in the street.

Come with a whoop and come with a call,
Come with a good will or not at all.
Up the ladder and down the wall,
A half-penny loaf will serve us all.

Spoken: You find milk, and I'll find flour,
And we'll have a pudding in half an hour.

16 Mary Had a Little Lamb

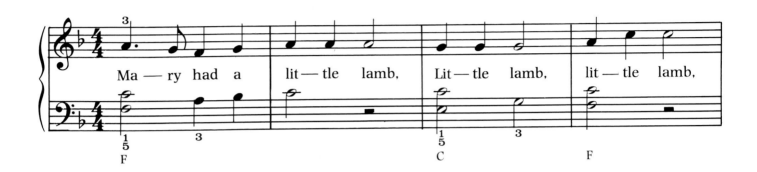

Ma — ry had a | lit — tle lamb, | Lit — tle lamb, | lit — tle lamb,

F   C   F

Verses 2, 3, 4

Ma — ry had a | lit — tle lamb, Its | fleece was white as | snow.

F   C⁷   F

And everywhere that Mary went,   It followed her to school one day,
Mary went, Mary went,   School one day, school one day,
Everywhere that Mary went,   Followed her to school one day,
The lamb was sure to go.   That was against the rule.

It made the children laugh and play
Laugh and play, laugh and play,
Made the children laugh and play,
To see a lamb at school.

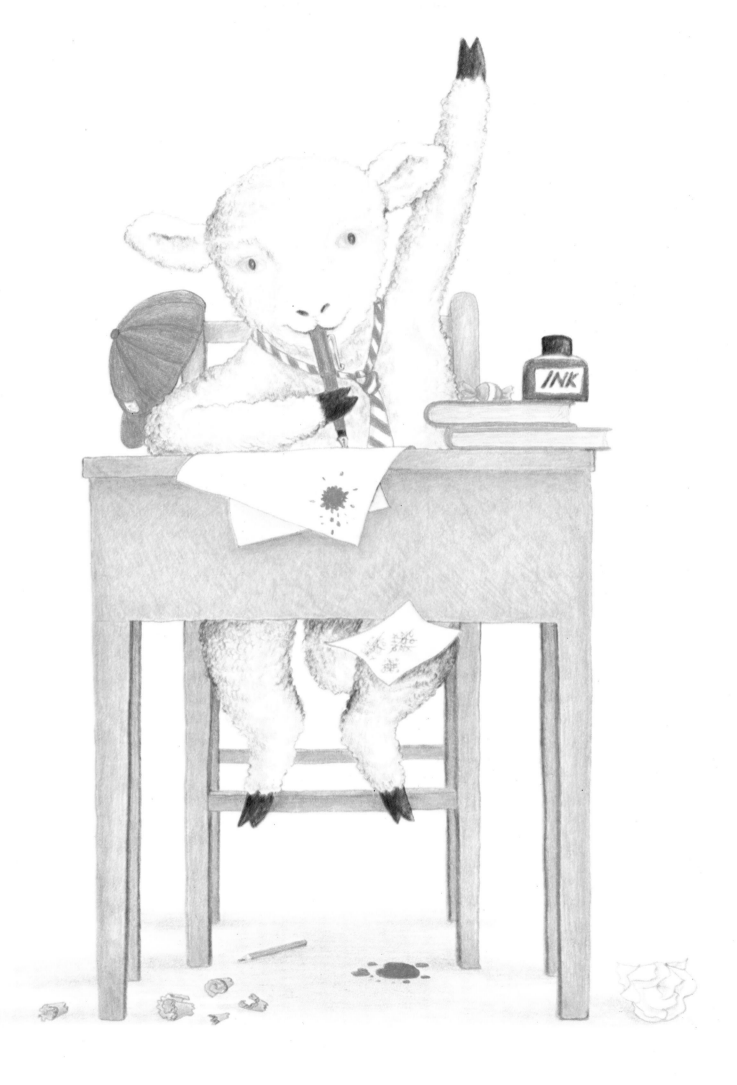

17 Rock-a-Bye Baby

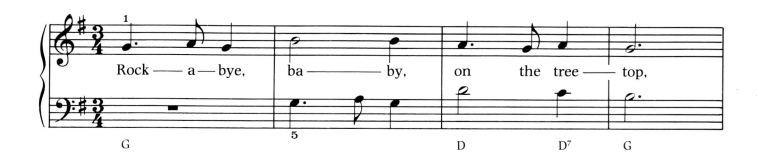

Rock — a — bye, ba — — by, on the tree — top,

G · · · · · · · · · · · · · · · · · · · D · · D⁷ · G

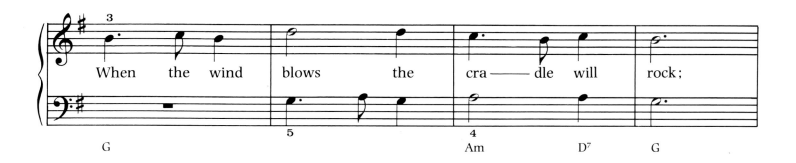

When the wind blows the cra — dle will rock;

G · · · · · · · · · · · · · · · · · Am · · D⁷ · G

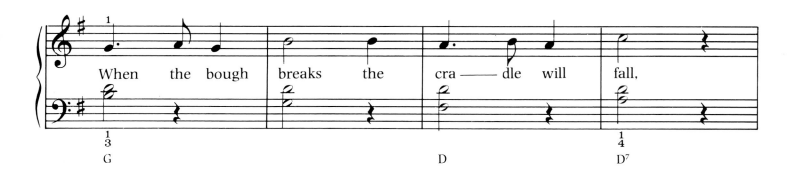

When the bough breaks the cra — dle will fall,

G · · · · · · · · · · · · · · · · · D · · · D⁷

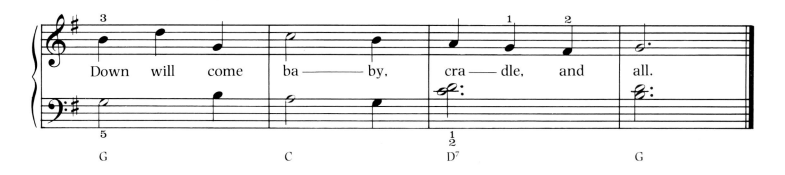

Down will come ba — — by, cra — dle, and all.

G · · · · · · · · C · · · · · · · D⁷ · · · · · · G

18 *Little Jack Horner*

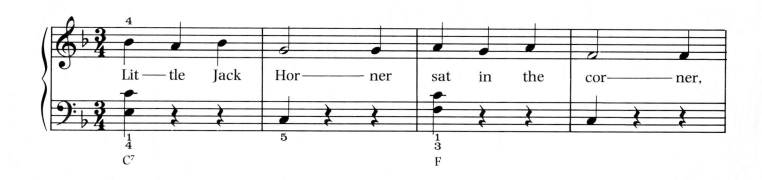

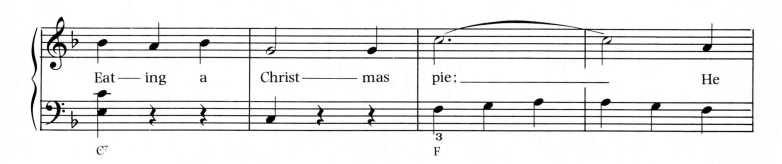

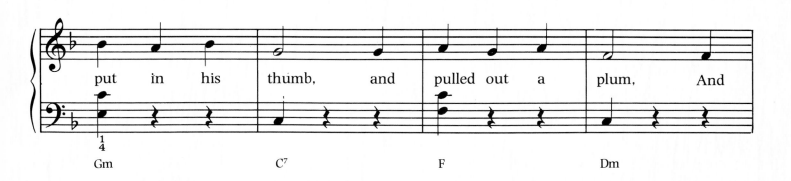

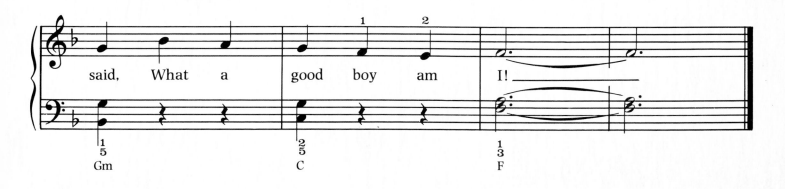

19   *Polly Put the Kettle On*

Pol — ly   put   the   ket — tle   on,   Pol — ly   put   the   ket — tle   on,

G

C⁶

D

Pol — ly   put   the   ket — tle   on, We'll   all   have   tea.

G

C   D   G

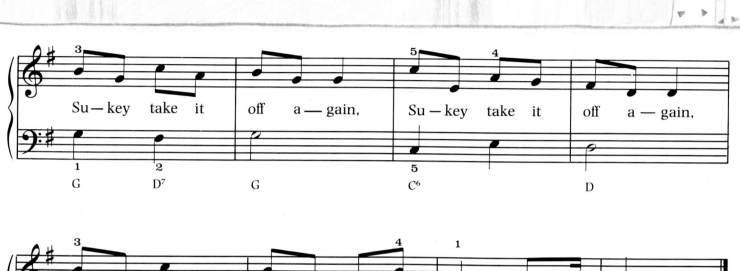

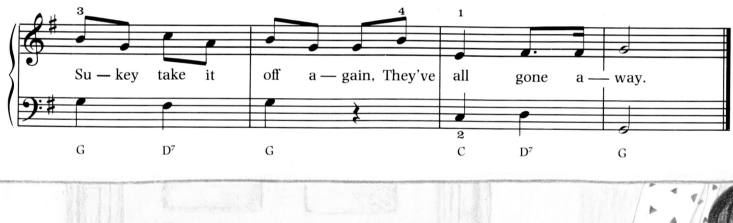

20 Humpty Dumpty

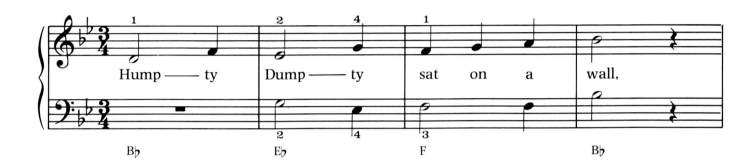

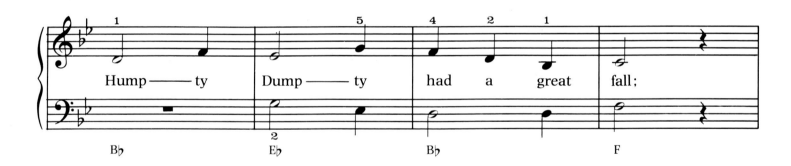

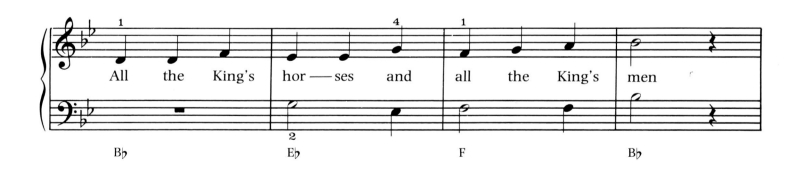

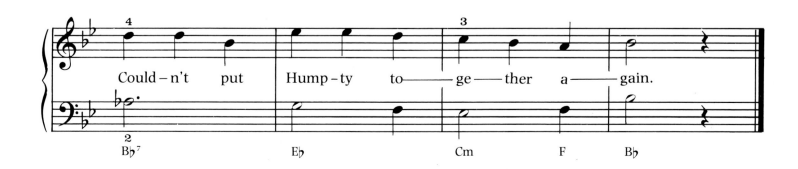

21 Little Bo-Peep

Lit——tle Bo——Peep has lost her sheep, And

F   C

does——n't know where ____ to find them;

F   F/C   C

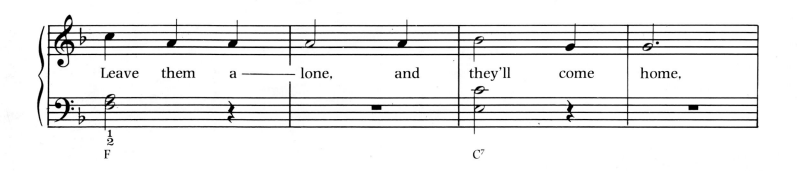

Leave them a————lone, and they'll come home,

F   C⁷

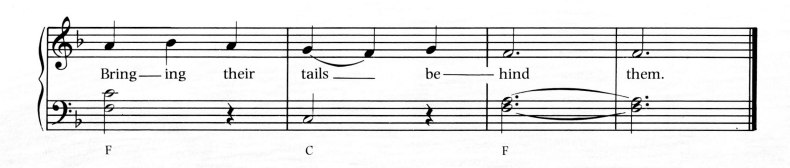

Bring——ing their tails ____ be——hind them.

F   C   F

Little Bo-Peep fell fast asleep,
And dreamt she heard them bleating;
But when she awoke, she found it a joke,
For they were still a-fleeting.

Then up she took her little crook,
Determined for to find them;
She found them indeed, but it made her heart bleed,
For they'd left their tails behind them.

It happened one day, as Bo-Peep did stray
Into a meadow hard by,
There she espied their tails side by side,
All hung on a tree to dry.

She heaved a sigh, and wiped her eye,
And over the hillocks went rambling,
And tried what she could, as a shepherdess should,
To tack again each to its lambkin.

22 Three Blind Mice

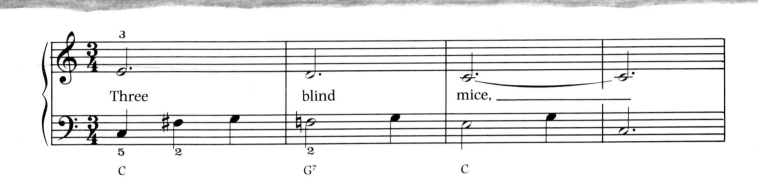

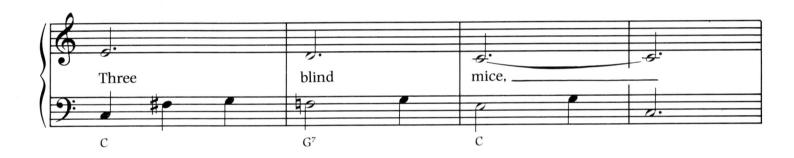

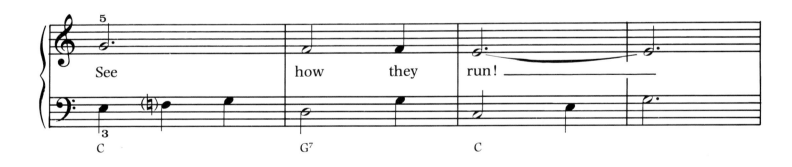

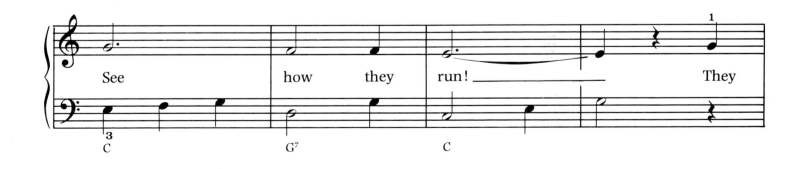

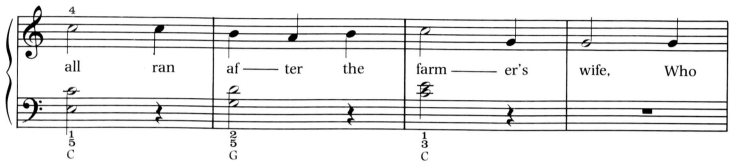

all   ran   af —— ter   the   farm —— er's   wife,   Who

C   G   C

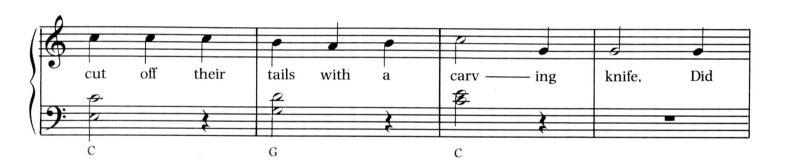

cut   off   their   tails   with   a   carv —— ing   knife,   Did

C   G   C

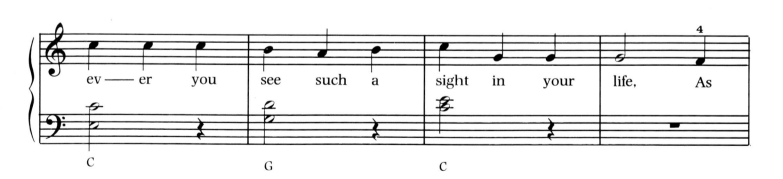

ev —— er   you   see   such   a   sight   in   your   life,   As

C   G   C

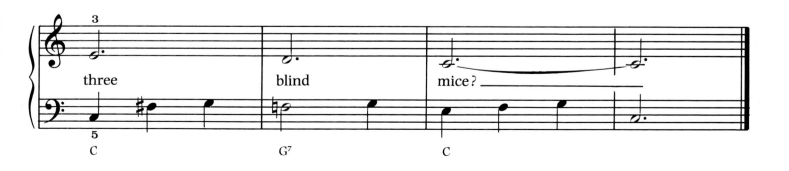

three   blind   mice? _____

C   G⁷   C

23 Mary, Mary, Quite Contrary

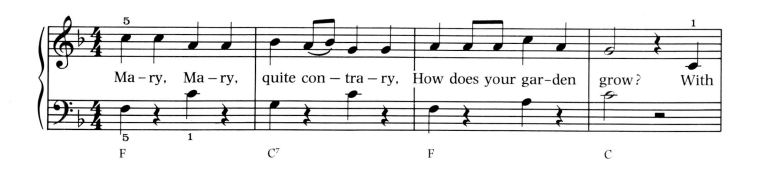

Ma – ry, Ma – ry, quite con – tra – ry, How does your gar – den grow? With

F   C⁷   F   C

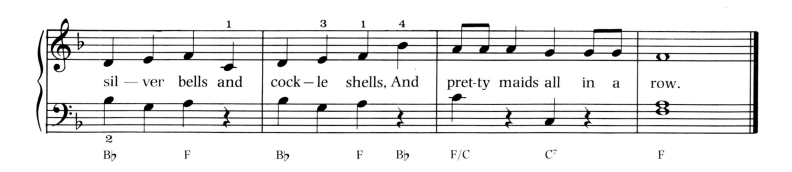

sil — ver bells and cock — le shells, And pret-ty maids all in a row.

B♭   F   B♭   F   B♭   F/C   C⁷   F

24 Cock-a-Doodle Doo!

Cock — a — doo — dle — doo! _____ My

D

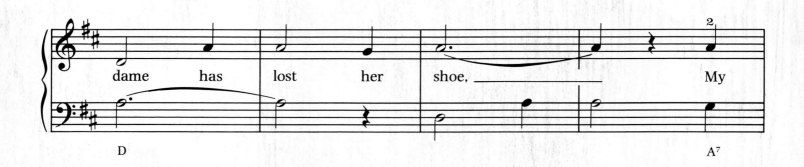

dame has lost her shoe, _____ My

D   A⁷

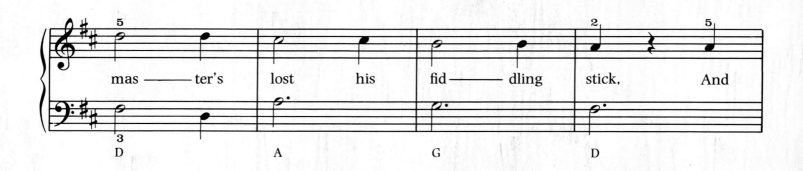

mas — ter's lost his fid — dling stick, And

D   A   G   D

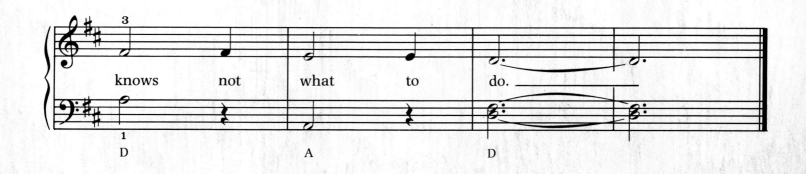

knows not what to do. _____

D   A   D

Cock-a-doodle-doo!
What is my dame to do?
Till master finds his fiddling stick,
She'll dance without her shoe.

Cock-a-doodle-doo!
My dame has found her shoe,
And master's found his fiddling stick,
Sing doodle-doodle-doo.

Cock-a-doodle-doo!
My dame will dance with you,
While master fiddles his fiddling stick,
For dame and doodle-doo.

25 *Baa, Baa, Black Sheep*

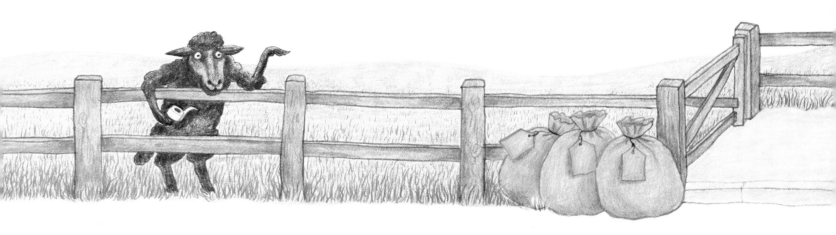

26 Hot Cross Buns

Hot cross buns!   Hot cross buns!   One a penny, two a penny, Hot cross buns!

F C F   C F   Bb   F/C C F

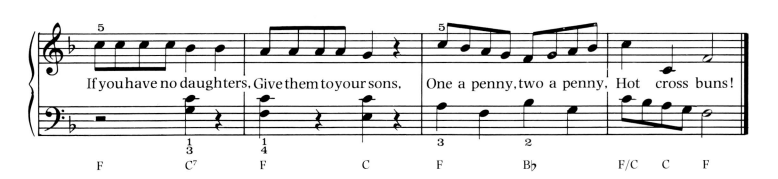

If you have no daughters, Give them to your sons,   One a penny, two a penny, Hot   cross buns!

F   C⁷   F   C   F   Bb   F/C   C   F

The Bakery

HOT CROSS BUNS

27 Goosey, Goosey Gander

28 Hey! Diddle, Diddle

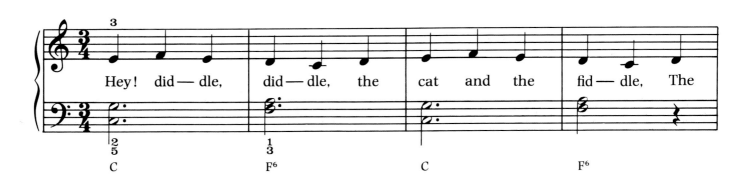

Hey! did — dle, did — dle, the cat and the fid — dle, The

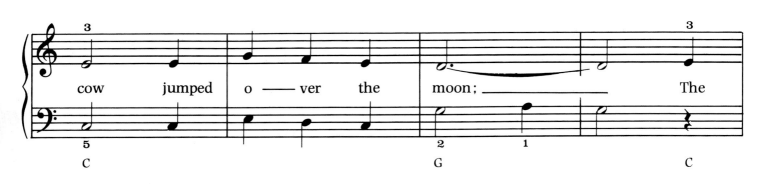

cow jumped o — ver the moon; _____ The

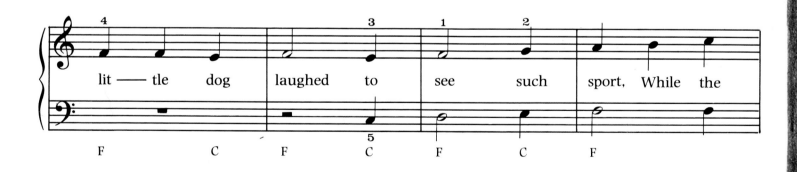

lit —— tle   dog   laughed   to   see   such   sport,   While   the

F   C   F   C   F   C   F

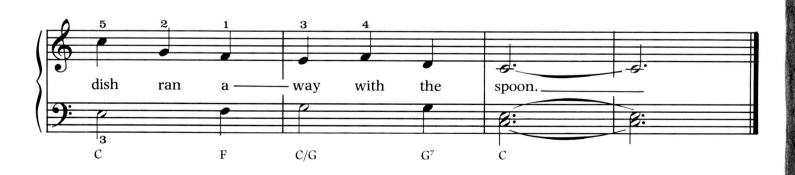

dish   ran   a ——— way   with   the   spoon. _____

C   F   C/G   G⁷   C

Fingering chart for guitar chords used in this book

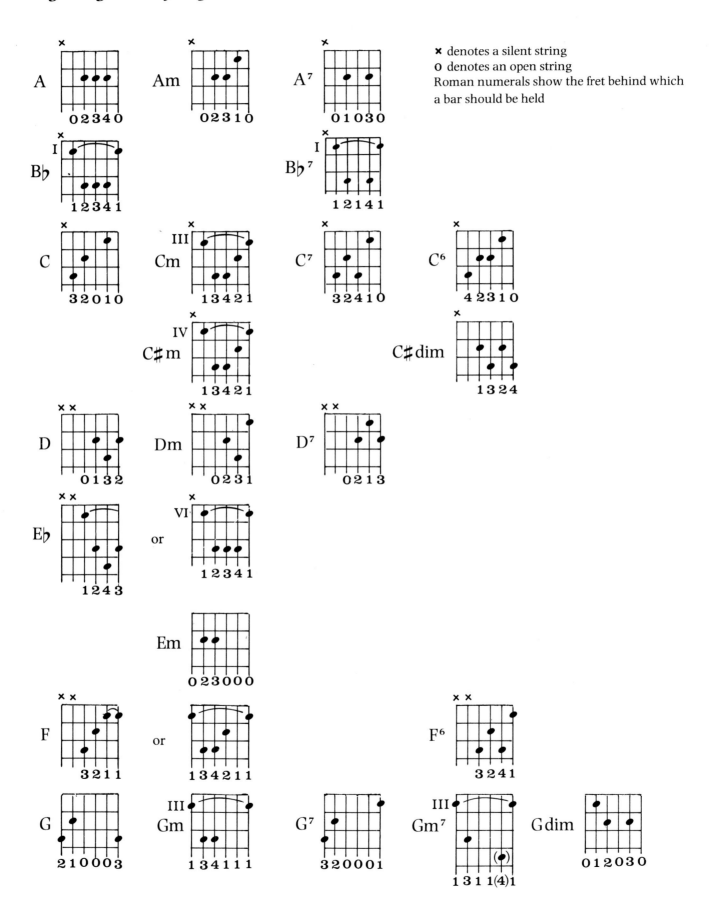

x denotes a silent string
o denotes an open string
Roman numerals show the fret behind which
a bar should be held